Simple Face Colouring Book

All rights are reserved Luka Poe. 2025

No part of this publication may be reproduced, stored in a retrieval system, or transmitted in any form or by any means, electronic, mechanical, photocopying, recording, or otherwise, without prior permission.

Welcome to the Simple Face Colouring Book!

This isn't just any coloring book — it's a journey through British culture, music, and legends, with a modern twist. Inside, you'll find bold, iconic faces that have shaped history, inspired generations, and rocked the world. From rock stars and royalty to literary legends and rebels, each illustration is waiting for your personal touch to bring it to life.

But don't expect boring, realistic portraits — this book is all about style, attitude, and creativity. Thick outlines and bold designs make it easy and fun to color, while the expressive faces invite you to experiment with colors, textures, and ideas.

Whether you're here for punk rock vibes, royal elegance, or a bit of British mystery, this book is designed to let you unleash your inner artist.

A Few Tips Before You Start:

No rules, just creativity! There's no right or wrong way to color these pages.

Use whatever tools you love — markers, crayons, colored pencils, or even digital coloring apps.

Add your own flair! Feel free to add extra details, backgrounds, or quotes to make each piece unique.

grab your colors, turn up the music, and get ready to rock and color your way through British history with a modern, artistic twist!

Enjoy the ride and remember:

"Art is the most intense mode of individualism the world has ever known." – Oscar Wilde

Now, it's time to color your own legend!

Born to Stand Out!

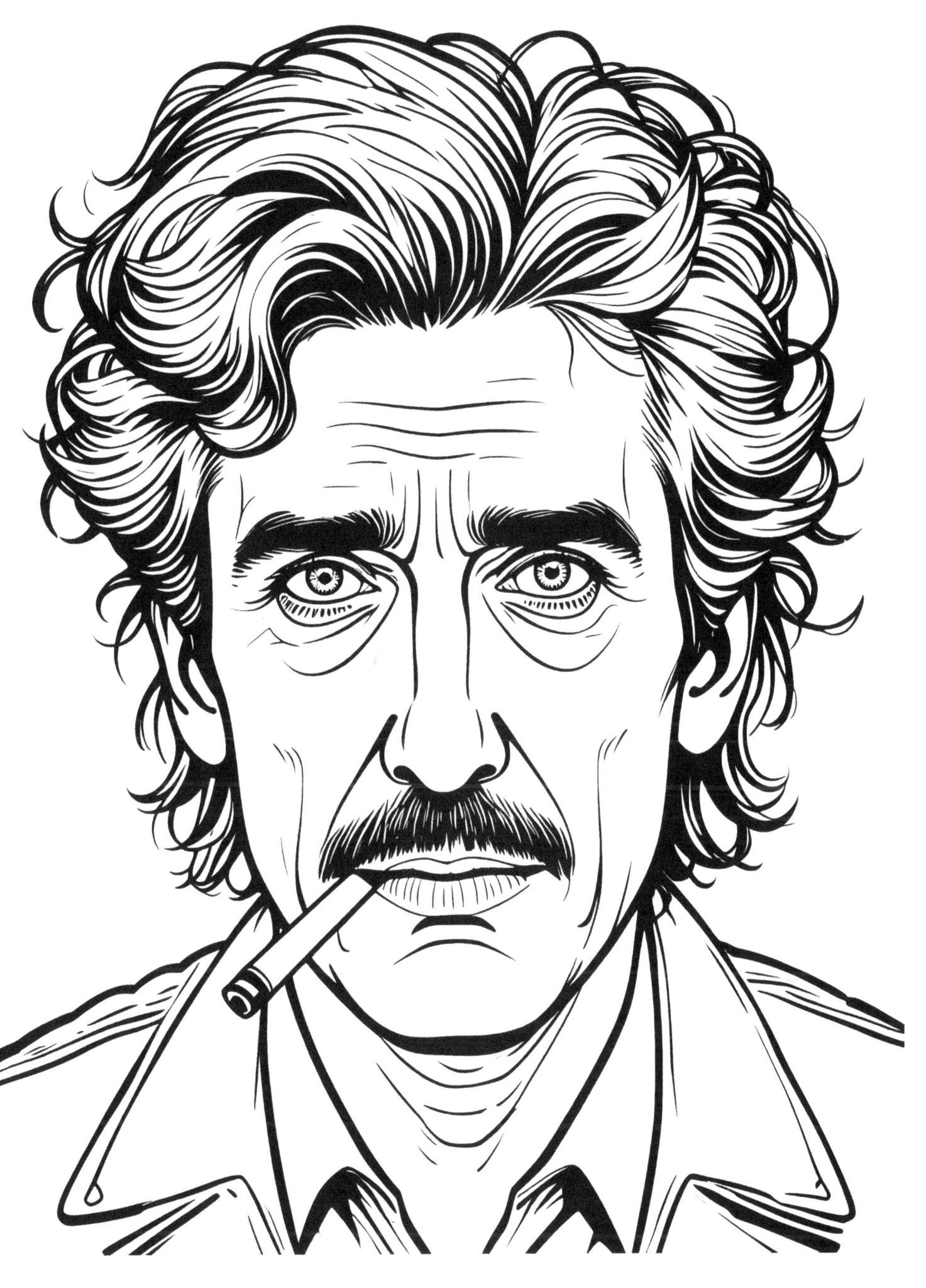

Stay Fierce!

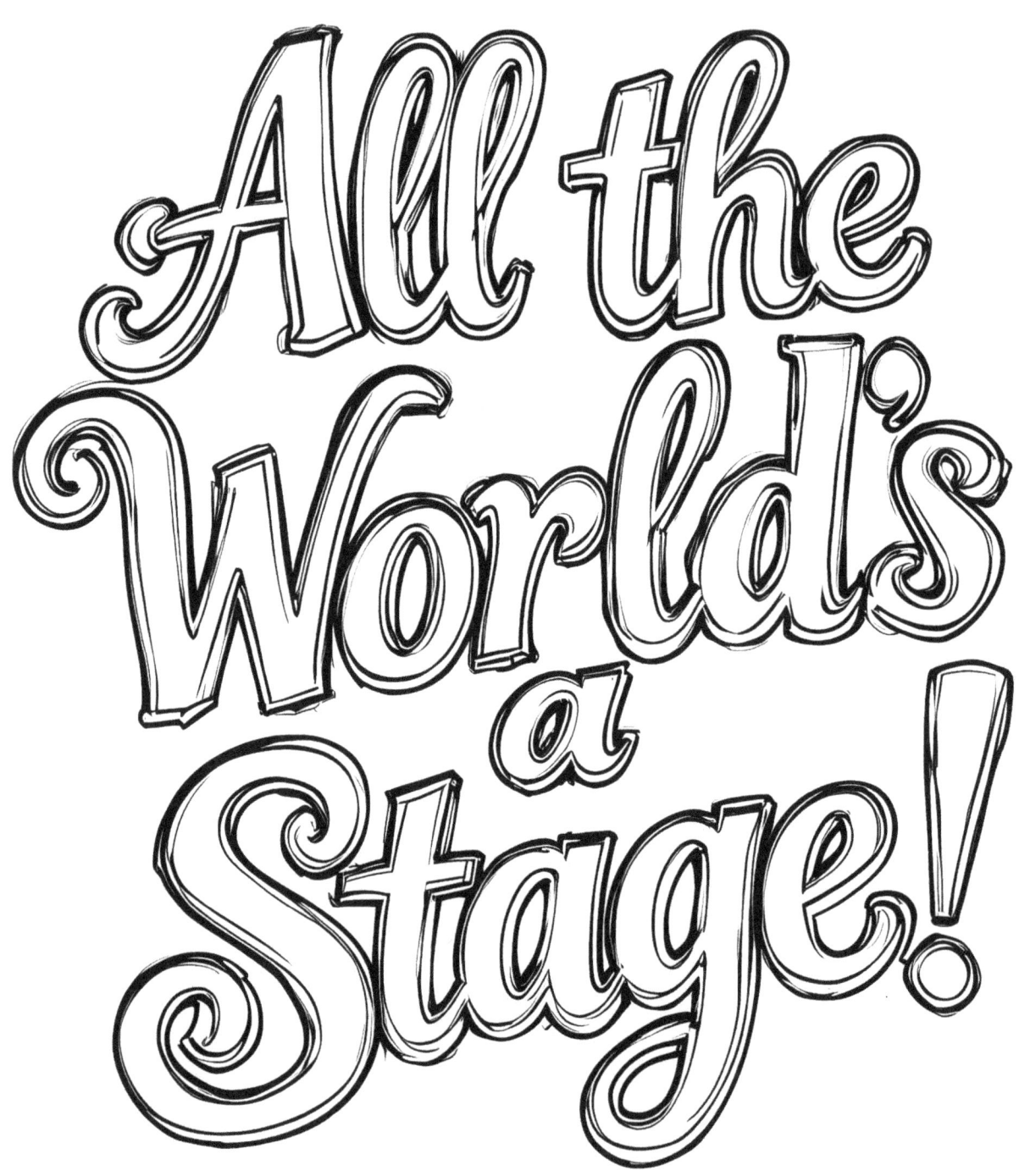

Crown Yourself with Confidence!

Stay Magical!

Timeless Beauty

Smoke & Shadows

Bold & & Beautiful

Queen of Style

Thank you for taking a colorful journey through the faces of British rock, literature, and culture! We hope you enjoyed bringing these iconic characters to life with your unique touch. Remember, every face tells a story — and you've added your own chapter to it.

Art is about expression, creativity, and having fun. Whether you colored inside the lines or took bold, artistic liberties, your work is one-of-a-kind. Just like the legends featured in this book, you've made your mark in a creative way!

We'd Love Your Feedback!

We'd be thrilled to hear about your experience with this coloring book. Your feedback not only helps us improve but also inspires future projects. If you have a moment, please consider leaving a review on Amazon or your favorite bookstore's website.

Did you have a favorite face? Did any of the designs resonate with you? Let us know!

🎸 Stay bold, stay creative, and keep coloring!

With love and creativity,

The Simple Face Colouring Book Team